Blessed Disillusionment

Seeing Through Ideas of Separation

Morgan Caraway

NON-DUALITY PRESS

BLESSED DISILLUSIONMENT

First published August 2011 by Non-Duality Press

Cover layout by John Gustard

Cover image is of light coming through a bottle wall built by Morgan and Mary Jane in their earthbag house near Asheville, NC.

Non-Duality Press | PO Box 2228 | Salisbury | SP2 2GZ
United Kingdom

ISBN: 978-0-9566432-9-2
www.non-dualitypress.com

Acknowledgements

This book is dedicated to my beloved Mary Jane, thank you for sharing this life. Thanks to my mother, Peggy Cottle and my father, Handly Caraway. Thanks to Linda Olk and James Galonsky for suggestions on this book. Thanks to Cliff Pollard for pointing out spelling errors. Thanks to John Wheeler for pointing so clearly at what is.

I am no authority; I am no smarter or holier than you. You don't need to read this book. The awareness seeing these words is perfectly complete right now and there is no need to continue. There is no information that you need to be awake. The "you" that needs something is absolutely unreal. Nothing can appear outside of wakefulness.

A clarification: when I say you (without quotations) in this book, I mean the awareness/presence/being you really are, NOT the thought image. When I say "you" I mean the apparent person.

This page contains all you need to be perfectly clear being as you are:

DISCLAIMER

In this book, our reality as being is what's being discussed. In appearance, Advaita isn't a justification to behave any way you want, to despoil the environment or act in a self-centered way. With the seeing of the self idea (ego) as non-existent, the destructive behaviors generated by the idea of separation should cease. This approach doesn't mean you should just say "Screw it" and not act intelligently with whatever arises. As John Wheeler (a very direct writer on this topic) told me, the idea that the appearance isn't important would be a value judgment and a misunderstanding of the core message. The essence of this is that there is no separation at all. All ideas of division are just that—ideas, with no reality other than as thoughts arising within awareness.

Nothing in this book is meant to imply that you shouldn't care if your family gets run over by a steam roller because you're *so detached*. It doesn't mean that you should stand frozen like a statue, not daring to even blink when flies crawl on your eyes, because "No one ever does anything anyway..." If there is the appearance of an abusive relationship or strife, it doesn't mean you shouldn't try to extract yourself from such situations. It just means that any psychological suffering that is experienced is based on a misconception that one is a separate person, apart from life.

I AM

If I was not, no experience could arise.

The thought “I am” is not what I am.

I am that which is prior to thought, which is its precondition.

I have never been limited, no borders impinge on me.

In my clarity, impressions and thoughts arise.

Some of these thoughts pretend to describe me.

Other thoughts reference these images.

Being is never sullied by appearances.

Our nature is freedom, we only suffer in thought.

In reality, oneness is all that ever appears.

There isn’t anyone who “gets this” and “doesn’t get it”.

There is only this.

Thoughts of confusion and separation will pass and

this will still be—thoughts couldn't appear without this.

THE WORD IS NOT "THE THING"

In this experience that could be called "my life", there has been a tendency to cling to ideas and mistake them for the essential. There can be the idea: "Now I've got it." And, with concepts that have been accepted as the truth in tow, one carries on until it is seen that the ideas are utterly impermanent.

The words aren't really important. They aren't reality or truth. The real is that in which these words appear.

What is ever-present in our experience? This is what all the talk about non-duality is trying to point at. That which comes and goes obviously isn't what you are. Words are transient—they are destined for dissolution. What do words and every other perception arise in? You don't need me to tell you. Awareness is the ground and being of everything, it is what you are.

Advaita as a conceptual understanding is a pointless belief system, as are all others—you don't need to believe to *be*. "Neti, neti…", "Not this, not that", just means that when you take every thing away, what is left?

Thought (mind) is the storyteller of life. No story

told has ever been true, be it the Bible, *War and Peace* or the personal story. My favorite form of fiction is biography. How can you tell if something is a story? If it is made up of words, thoughts or images. Though many stories have a tremendous sense of drama and urgency, they appear in serene, seeing emptiness. This is what is real. This is obvious right now.

IMAGINE

Imagine the most amazing spiritual experience you can.

Imagine that your favorite saint or guru comes down from heaven and happily declares: "You're enlightened!"

Imagine that all of your chakras blaze with an inner light brighter than a billion suns and that you radiate eternal bliss into the far reaches of the universe. OK?

Now what?

All experience is fleeting. That is the defining characteristic of any experience. That's why seeking after an experience to find yourself is futile. Any event will happen and fade, leaving what is. It is the "what is", the abiding reality, that Advaita is concerned with. That reality is what you are. (The word "Advaita" is just a very basic pointer meaning "Not two".)

Though you are the source of appearance, you aren't bound by any of the forms that appear. In truth, nothing exists outside of you. There is no body, mind or universe other than as impressions registering in timeless being. Only the being is real, the appearances are like a mirage. Just as heat creates the mirage and not vice versa, consciousness gives rise to the appearance and not the other way around. The appearance *is* consciousness appearing. This is easily observable in direct experience. In the absence of consciousness (such as in deep sleep) what can appear?

There are not things, there is only nothing or not-a-thing. This nothingness isn't dead and dull, it is pure sentience. It is the core of everything that can be considered an experience. Without it, there could be no appearance.

As Nisargadatta Maharaj and others have pointed out, the problem—only in a relative and not absolute sense—encountered by timelessly appearing impressions, thoughts and beliefs that we mistakenly label "a person", is that some thoughts identify I, or the self sense, with the body and mind.

The body is not an object, just fluctuating perceptions that come and go in awareness. The mind isn't real, only presently appearing thoughts from which a thing called mind is surmised. Therefore, when we talk about the mind, body, world or whatever else, it gives credence to the idea that they are independent things, when, actually, they have no reality apart from consciousness.

When we talk about people or things there is an implied "apparent" before what we say. It would be pedantic and clumsy to say "apparent" every time one mentions someone or something in conversation but—as was stated before—there is no thing apart from *What Is.* Language implies distinctions where no division can be made.

NO OBJECT

Looking subjectively (through direct experience), what is seen?

There are all kinds of perceptions that arise and disappear on their own. There are thoughts that come into being and soon fade back into nothingness. There are sensations of a body, doing different activities; many viewpoints of it are seen—mostly just the arms, hands, feet, legs and, perhaps, torso (unless one looks in a mirror). There are impressions of what we call the world or universe—all types of varying experiences which come and go, not leaving a mark on the intangible presence that perceives them. Even consciousness appears in the morning, on waking, and vanishes each night in deep sleep.

What is aware of these constantly changing states and appearances?

If we have been taught to view the world objectively—as a collection of independent objects—we might answer: "It is my brain that registers all of these things." But that is just a story that we have been told.

From our direct experience, thought (the mind) isn't constant. Nor are what we label bodily or worldly impressions. Nor is even consciousness, that is: an awareness of things. In the lack of a seeming objective appearance, presence/awareness isn't conscious of itself (what separate self is there for it to be conscious of?). In this totally uncomplicated *be-ing,* there is ultimate peace and resting as all that one has ever been—no thing.

NO METHOD

There is no method to achieve "enlightenment". The idea that there is depends on two misconceptions.

1. The idea of a me that is apart from enlightenment.

2. The concept that enlightenment is a thing to have or not have.

The reality is that every experience and form appears in the clear light of being and that there has never been anyone or anything apart from that.

You can say "Neti, neti" until you pass out from oxygen deprivation. You can ask "Who am I?" for billions of years until the sun goes supernova, but that won't make you one infinitesimal bit more what you are than what you are right now.

Thought cannot understand this, nor does it need to. In the presence or absence of thought, *you are*. Watch your experience and you'll see all thoughts come and go. When thoughts are gone, you are still present. This is proof that your are not your thoughts.

NO TEACHER

Any teacher (in understanding one's true nature, the idea of teacher/student or guru/disciple is clearly dualistic) who offers something you can do to become who you already are is a used snake-oil salesperson or, at least, confused. How can you become more or less what you are? Such teachings seem to speak from and to an imaginary separate entity who, in actuality, is only a thought appearing in awareness.

There are some (apparently!) who say: "You should try to be more present. Silence your thoughts and merge into the now."

First off, who is the you to do these things—a thought image?

Secondly, where can one be apart from being? Where can a thought arise other than in presence right now. A thought has never arisen in anything other than present awareness—it's impossible.

One might think that these carrots on sticks keep thought spinning, whilst, all the while, this apparent drama unfolds in perfectly clear, undisturbed awareness.

There isn't a spiritual in club—those who have "gotten it" and those who haven't. You can't get or lose this—you *are* it.

Talking to (an apparent) someone who isn't mired in concepts, spiritual or otherwise, can be helpful. I called John Wheeler while reading his book, *You Were Never Born,* and brought up all of the concepts that I could and put them on the table. He proceeded to take the proverbial hammer out and smash them to bits (in a very gentle way). The burden of those ideas dropped as soon as their unreality was seen.

The key thing that John points at is undeniable present being. He also points at the unreality of the me image—the believed-in separate person.

NO WORDS

You don't need to hear any words or read any books to be what you are, this book included. The word is never the thing described. Usually, the less that is said the better. Being is so simple that words invariably make it seem more complicated than it is.

What can be simpler than oneness?

What can be more familiar than the natural presence that you are?

It is so intrinsic to every experience that we miss awareness and focus on the shifting, transient images that appear. It's understandable—not being an object, it can't be seen—one *is* it.

Usually, when this is first recognized, the thought may arise: "Oh, *that*—that can't be it." And seeking an amazing spiritual experience or a non-stop bliss buffet binge continues—wanting eternal happiness and all of that, not realizing the obvious fact that all feelings and thoughts are bound to fade. When they are gone, what I am will still be present.

Nothing will bring me closer to being what I am—no experience, no feeling, no meditation, no thought, no book, no belief, no vision, no prayer, no satsang, no dharma transmission, no guru, no teacher, no drug. There is no possible way to become what you are or be what you aren't. The reality of being is inescapable.

It doesn't matter which word is preferred: "awareness", "presence", "being", "God", "spirit", "noumenon", "Brahman", "the Tao", "love"—they all point at the same reality. You are this singular principle. Nothing exists apart from it. Nothing could appear to be without it. It is not-a-thing but *it is, you are, I am* (all saying the exact same thing).

NO SEEKER

There never has been anyone apart from being that could seek it. The seeker is just an image appearing in consciousness. The root of it is a belief that there is a separate entity that lacks something. When looked for, this "person" can't be found. It's like the old Zen story where the disciple goes to his master and says: "I'm having trouble with my mind." And the master says: "Well, put it here in front of me and I'll sort it out."

It's the same with the ego or seeker: when looked for, it's simply not around. All that is seen is space or openness in which passing thoughts and impressions appear.

NO ATMAN (INDIVIDUAL SOUL) APART FROM BRAHMAN (UNIVERSAL CONSCIOUSNESS)

To adherents of Advaita Vedanta:
"I am Brahman, the supreme, all-pervading like the ether, stainless, indivisible, unbounded, unmoved, unchanging. I have neither inside nor outside. I alone am. I am one without a second. What else is there to be known?"

"Brahman cannot be avoided, since it is everywhere. Brahman cannot be grasped, since it is transcendent. It cannot be contained since it contains all things. It is one without a second. In Brahman there is no diversity whatsoever."

—from Shankara's *Crest-Jewel of Discrimination*

How could Brahman, which is one without a second, have individual components called *Atman*? Why even speak of such a distinction? When that which cannot be described or divided is discussed, it seems to lead to the implication that there is, indeed, separation.

These attempted fragmentations of wholeness are simply thought descriptions and don't tell the truth. Any thing with identifiable properties and qualities is not what is being pointed at; this is how we know all of the words are false. Even the phrase "I am" is a needless complication of the profound simplicity of being.

Philosophy, whether religious or secular in nature, cannot break Brahman (oneness) apart to analyze it. Any attempt to do so ends up with a set of concepts being taken for reality, which they aren't. The real is that which is always present, and without which there would be no appearance of anything at all.

You can't know it as an idea; you can only know it as the truth of what you are.

More excerpts from *Crest-Jewel*:

"Brahman is supreme. He is the reality—the one without a second. He is pure consciousness, free from any taint. He is tranquility itself. He has neither beginning nor end. He does not change. He is joy forever."

"That Reality pervades the universe, but no one penetrates it. It alone shines. The universe shines with its reflected light."

"The sun's rays bring forth layers of cloud. By them, the sun is concealed; and so it appears that the clouds alone exist. In the same way, the ego, which is brought forth by the Atman (Brahman), hides the true nature of the Atman (Brahman); and so it appears that the ego alone exists."

"The waking state is only a prolonged dream. The phenomenal universe exists in the mind. In dreamless sleep, when the mind does not function, nothing exists. This is our universal experience. Man seems to be in bondage to birth and death. This is a fictitious creation of the mind, not a reality."

Don't let all of the talk of minds, egos, Atman and universes fool you—what is being pointed at is what is beyond all of these labels and is present right now; it is what is aware of reading these words, thoughts and bodily and worldly sensations. Without this undifferentiated awareness, there would be no experience.

"Both bondage and liberation are fictions of ignorance. They are not in the Atman. The Atman is infinite, without parts, beyond action. It is serene, stainless, pure. How can one imagine duality in Brahman, which is entire like the ether, without a second, the supreme reality?"

"There is neither birth nor death, neither bound nor aspiring soul, neither liberated soul nor seeker after liberation—this is the ultimate and absolute truth."

NO PROBLEM

Problems only seem to exist in appearance. The word "problem" is a label that thought puts on something that doesn't fit the image that arises of how something should be.

For the crystal-clear awareness that we are, there are no problems. Nothing sticks to it. It isn't subject to the dream-like world of form. Regardless of what happens in appearance, it remains unblemished and untouched. It isn't that it's *above* or *apart* from what appears, it's just that the images that arise within it are transitory and ephemeral. As you are timeless, omniscient being, why worry about an image or a thought that's just passing through?

The idea that there is being on one side and thoughts on the other is also false. There is nothing apart from that which I am. Nothing can appear to arise in anything other than *What Is.* No matter what may seem to happen in appearance, no matter how tragic or unfair it may seem, the timeless, indestructible being that you are is absolutely unmarred as it is immutable.

Pure Advaita is the easiest thing in the world. There is nothing to be achieved, there is no one to achieve it and, lastly, there is no world; there is only timeless awareness appearing as everything and nothing. How much effort does it take to *be*?

NO SHIT

This is right here and nowhere else. It's so painfully obvious. It's the only principle that's remained constant through the appearance of a life. It was there before the birth of an apparent person and it will be unchanged after what we call death. It is pure undivided being and it is the only thing that can truly be called "I".

This isn't special knowledge or a rare understanding that is being talked about. It's completely ordinary. It's also kind of magical—the nothing that appears as everything. No one can claim to have this while others don't. It is the key ingredient of any experience or perception.

When I say nothing, I'm not talking about a nihilistic void but the living light of awareness. It is the very essence of life, not an empty, cold, barren darkness, as thought might imagine.

In the appearance, you are told certain things as you grow up. One of these things is that you are a "person" living in a "world". You are told your name and that you are a separate being, responsible for your actions. Later, you're told more things that add to this confusion. These things that we are taught often get held onto as beliefs. We forget how to look at our direct experience and knowing gives way to knowledge.

There is the belief that we know so many things but almost all of it is hearsay. We're told that we're physical beings in a material universe, that we're independent of the rest of creation and choose our own destiny. We're told that we have a physical structure called the brain inside of our skulls and that that's the source of consciousness. We're told all kinds of things, but, if we look at our direct experience, there is a cognizant space or emptiness in which all sorts of impressions and thoughts appear and disappear. There are perceptions that get labeled "the body", "the mind", "the world", giving seeming validity to the idea of separate things, but they all arise in undivided awareness.

Time is also only an idea. Actually, there has never been any time apart from the present. Ideas of past and future only arise now. Whenever you look, it's always now; time is just an abstraction of timelessness in thought. I knew a guy who had a clock that instead of having numbers at the hour marks just said "now"—how true!

Trying to be more present is like water trying to be wetter. Everything arises presently, even the idea that there is someone who isn't present.

IF THERE IS NO SEPARATE SELF, WHY DOESN'T MY LIFE SEEM PERFECT?

First off, the idea of perfection is a thought image. One apparent situation or thing is labeled "perfect" and another, "flawed". Without contrast, there can be no appearance. Positive and negative, pleasure and pain, happiness and sadness—in the seeming manifestation, there can't be one without the other. As in all, there isn't a real duality in the opposites, it's just more distinctions imagined in that which is whole and undivided.

The seasons flow naturally into one another. To call summer "good" and winter "bad" means you will embrace the warm weather and suffer when it's cold. Without the mental label, it simply is what it is and one can be at peace with all of it. It is the same with all aspects of life. Waiting for reality to become like a concept says it should be is failing to appreciate the present moment, in all of its beauty and ugliness.

If an apparent person stubs their apparent toe, it's going to apparently hurt. If joy can be felt, sadness can be felt. Anything can appear in life and thought is in the habit of labeling what arises as either good, bad or indifferent. The things labeled "good" are sought after and those called "bad" are avoided but, inevitably, both must arise in appearance—*that* is what allows appearance to appear!

Any preference for one or the other will cause apparent suffering because the opposite is unavoidable. (The ideas of opposites and multiplicity are only in thought.)

The people who strive the hardest for constant happiness seem to be the most tortured because no thought, feeling or sensation is permanent. If it is seen that one is the spacious awareness in which all forms appear and dissolve then one can be at peace with what arises. Every thing is fleeting so why get hung up on it?

The idea of the separate self leads directly to apparent suffering. If there is the concept that one is someone who can do something then struggling will arise within thought. The ego is ultimately nothing more than an unexamined assumption. If looked for, no ego will ever be found—it doesn't exist. Take a look! Also, there is no separate self to get rid of the idea of a separate self!

I AM, THEREFORE THINKING ARISES

Descartes had it wrong.

Thinking arises in being, not the other way around. What awareness does a thought have? What thoughts can appear outside of consciousness? None, absolutely none.

Being is the source of all appearances, including thought. Often in "spiritual" circles, there is the idea that thought is detrimental to presence. On the contrary, thought can only arise in presence.

Everything that appears is the light of awareness patterning. Though thought imagines that the patterns have their own independent existence, they are all only that light, including thought.

NO NEED

Multiplying words is not necessary. There is no need to stop thought. It doesn't matter if an apparent person is earnest or has any other qualities that seem to make them a candidate for awakening. You are perfectly complete being right now, regardless of what appears. For any thing to appear, you must *be*. All thoughts of a limited, separate individual are simply concepts registering in present, boundless awareness. Take a look.

There is no need to emulate the saints. As appearance, they are no more or less sacred than you. As *being*, they *are* you. No matter what appears, there is only ever One and it is not-a-thing.

The appearance of every activity that can be imagined—chanting, praying, meditation, sex, buying groceries, arguing, drinking milk, digging a ditch, reading—arises in undivided, perfectly clear being. Accompanying these appearances, there is often a thought story of a person who is doing said actions but, actually, the same thing (no thing) is happening everywhere (there is really only here—"here" being where awareness is).

There is only awareness. (What I am)

There is only here. (Where I am)
There is only now. (When I am)
There is only I. (Who I am)
All is summed up by "I am".

All ideas of other times and other things are only thoughts that appear in what I am. This you are also.

IDEAS OF GOD AND DIVINITY

Unfortunately, at least for the apparent seeker, most ideas of God that one comes across in life are entirely dualistic. Some examples of these types of ideas might be:

"I am a solid body with a brain inside living in a material universe and there is an external God to whom I can pray and ask for help."

"I am a physical being, but, within my body, there exists God."

"I have been given a separate existence and free will by God so that I can be tested to see if I am worthy of being in His presence for eternity or if I should suffer unending punishment."

"I am a separate soul that is evolving through countless lifetimes and will eventually reach perfection and unity with God."

"If my behavior is good in this life, next life I'll be reborn in a form that is more conducive to enlightenment."

"God is trying to call me to heaven and the Devil is trying to call me to hell."

"Every separate person has a tiny bit of the light of God in them."

"There is no God, only a material universe which we are inhabitants of."

"God created this world and everything in it and then left us to work out our own destiny."

As can be seen, all of these beliefs involve an apparent entity that is apart from God or being. Has there ever been such a thing? Usually there is an implication that, if certain requirements are met, one will get closer to God. Can one get closer to what one is?

THE BASICS

Thoughts arise.
Sensations are felt.
Things are perceived.
All of these are experiences.
For there to be experience, you must be aware.
Awareness gives rise to thoughts, sensations and impressions.
There is nothing apart from the sentient space of being.
I AM.

WHATEVER

Whatever can be held can be lost.
Whatever can be remembered can be forgotten.
Whatever can be made can be broken.
Whatever can be desired can be feared.
Whatever can be found can be hidden.
Whatever can be helped can be hurt, but only in appearance.
In truth, there are no conditions.
Being can never be other than it is.
Being birthless, it cannot die.
Being timeless, it cannot end.
Being boundless, it cannot be caged.
Being formless, it cannot dissolve.
Being self-shining, it cannot be dimmed.
Being unseen, it cannot disappear.
Being empty, it appears as everything.
Being everything, it cannot be lost.

A PARABLE

Two friends, who were seekers after truth, heard of a wise man who lived on top of the tallest mountain in the world. After discussing, they agreed that he would definitely know the answers to all of their questions. They decided to go see him.

They took weeks to prepare for their journey, making sure they had everything they'd need. It took them nearly a month to reach the foot of the mountain, and, eager to learn the secrets of the universe, they hastily started climbing.

They climbed for what seemed like years. As they approached the summit, the air got thinner and each step was a grueling endurance test.

When they neared the top, there was a full-scale blizzard going on. Through the flurries, they could make out the shape of an ancient-looking bearded man sitting in the lotus position—it was *him*! They couldn't contain their excitement; soon all of their questions would be answered.

With the last of their strength, they climbed swiftly towards him. As they got closer, they could see that his eyes were shut and that he was silently meditating.

As they were within arm's length of him, they were just about to start asking their questions when he opened his eyes and said: "Hey, either one of you guys know how the hell to get down from here? I came up here years ago looking for a wise man and got stuck!"

In being, there is absolutely no hierarchy. It is impossible for anyone to be closer to or further from is-ness than anyone else. There are no experts who can teach you how to be what you already are. Attempting to teach *being* would be like trying to teach a fish how to breathe water—completely redundant.

Teachers who act like they have something that you don't are deluding themselves and, if their spiel is believed, fooling you too.

Awareness wasn't the possession of the Buddha, or ancient Chinese masters, or Jesus, or yogis, or Zen patriarchs, or Osho, or Eckhart Tolle, or Nisargadatta, or the Dalai Lama, or any other image of an "enlightened being" that can be imagined. Everything arises in the same consciousness. We (I am) are the source of that consciousness—the absolute. The absolute is aware of even the coming and going of consciousness.

That is not to make a distinction between

consciousness and the absolute—consciousness is just one of the states that arises within it, as unconsciousness is. The absolute is not a state. It is, as the name implies, all-encompassing. Every state and every thing apparently rises and sets within it. In truth, it is always as it is—unchanged and undiminished. There is no reality apart from that and we are that.

AN IDEA CANNOT KNOW

Being is present right now and now is all there is. Within being appear perceptions. Right now there is the appearance of words. These words can in no way affect the presence in which they arise. Looking directly, this is beyond simple. Trying to look through concepts is impossible. A concept cannot describe that which is non-conceptual, although it can be used as a pointer. An idea cannot see. Only being sees and knows. All there is is this knowing. We are this.

It is a great relief to know that one is nothing, especially after an apparent time of identification with the thought story. Being "something" would be a very precarious position if it was possible—"you" could get broken and you'd be bound for ultimate dissolution. All forms arise and fade. Luckily, we are the formless and all that appears is only the play/appearance of being. Not a problem!

DIRECT KNOWING

Only the fact of one's being can be known directly. All knowledge after that is conceptual. Knowing (what we are) is confused with knowledge (what we think we are). Knowing is our nature and easier and more automatic than breathing. You can't not know. I am: it doesn't get any simpler than the naked fact of being. Concepts arise in this knowing and, if they're accepted as reality, they become knowledge. This knowledge is really only ignorance, though—none of it is true. Only being exists and it cannot be conceptually divided.

Thought/words, being a system of symbols, cannot describe the real. Thought, in attempting to understand, ends up dissecting and compartmentalizing so the inherent wholeness is missed. If thoughts are seen as merely appearances that arise and set in presence, then there is no apparent problem. It is only if they are taken to be truth that the simplicity of oneness seems to get extraordinarily complex. It isn't. There is only what is, the presence indicated by the phrase: "I am". All ideas of duality are thought's interpretation of appearance, an illusory description of a mirage.

I would say "Abide in being." But there's really no

other option, as being is all there is and there is no one apart from it to do or not do anything.

"I am" is a concept and, therefore, unreal—it's what it is pointing to that is important.

Drop the words and what is left?

"WHAT ABOUT ALL OF THE SUFFERING IN THE WORLD?"

"What about Hitler, Charles Manson and Dick Cheney? How do you explain all of the evil in the world? What kind of God would allow such things to happen?"

Here's the short answer: nothing is happening.

An explanation:
All that's real is self-illuminating, timeless awareness. It's impossible for concepts to explain something so real that its dream appears as the universe of matter. Within this sentience appear images. Some of these scenes depict villains and foul deeds. Others show actions and beings that would be considered heroic—darkness and light—contrast. As was said before: no contrast, no appearance.

While, seemingly, titanic dramas are played out, in truth the non-dual clarity of being is what all arises in. Without presence, there would be no possibility of an apparent manifestation. The characters who make their entrances and exits on the stage of awareness are none other than that self-same awareness wearing masks of form. Nothing is created or destroyed. Being abides regardless of what seems to happen.

For non-material and formless awareness, death is not possible. Only appearances come and go, not the absolute which is the essence of everything and nothing.

"WHAT HAPPENS AFTER DEATH?"

How the hell would *I* know?

The only things that can be said with certainty are that the "self" that would die is just a fictional character and that whatever is the case during the appearance of life will still be so after death: whole, undivided being will be all that's happening.

If appearance/consciousness ceases then it seems it would be impossible to believe in any form of duality or separation.

To what we are, life isn't a problem and neither is death. Only apparent forms are subject to such things and we are not forms.

One might wonder what happened before birth and what will happen after death. In actuality, no one was born, no one will die and the duration in between is purely conceptual. It is, of course, always only now and, regardless of appearances and thoughts to the contrary, I am only what I am. In this timeless presence, time, space and the world of form appear and fade effortlessly.

NO BELIEF NECESSARY

To see what is being discussed here, no belief is necessary. Direct experience will show all that needs to be known. Adhering to concepts is pointless. They are bound to fade and can't possibly describe the real. Anything that can be described by thought is an illusion. Only the unnamable is real.

I used to have a bumper sticker that read: "Don't believe everything you think". I would go a step further and say, don't believe *anything* you think, especially that there is a you who thinks!

Isn't it obvious that you are aware and present right now? What could be seen or felt outside of that awareness? The forms that arise are just a mirage generated by the heat and light of being. They appear within and because of you, but don't define you.

When one identifies with thought and it is believed to be generated by a "me", life seems impossibly complicated. Thought describes billions and trillions of things. The cosmos that is imagined is a fragmented and crowded place, teeming with unrelated and alien objects. Also, it imagines an inner existence that is easily as perplexing as the outer"(there is no inner and outer: another false duality). The thoughts that arise out of being-ness are seen as belonging to "me" and, therefore, there is an attempt to keep them within certain limits (defined by the self-image). Being doesn't have to color in the lines so there can often appear a struggling with thoughts as they fall outside of the acceptable boundaries of the me concept.

Whatever thinking arises is OK—it isn't what you are nor can you (also only a thought) control it, so why try to alter it at all? All appearances (including thought) arise and dissolve without any interference from an idea of me. All there is is flawless clarity in which thoughts and impressions arise and pass.

Please don't believe anything said in this book—it wont do a bit of any kind of good. Look for yourself. Everything that needs to be known is present now: you are the knowing.

Ramana Maharshi pointed out that the first idea is the self idea. The first idea is "I am": the conceptual statement of being. With the arising of the concept of "me" as a body and mind comes also the "not me"—the world/universe. This is the first and primary duality imagined by thought. It is also an utter falsity. Only the absolute is real and it is not divided. Self, space and time are just ideas that arise within its brilliant, spacious, perceptive presence.

NO EFFORT

Everything arises spontaneously. Superimposed over this is the *I* thought, claiming ownership and taking responsibility. The *I* is an afterthought. Functioning takes place perfectly without it. The appearance of the body eats and craps and walks and has sex without any help from an idea of a me. If the self concept arises, that's just an appearance in being too, masquerading as something apart.

When the *me* idea isn't believed in, thoughts and impressions still arise, some of which reference a supposed separate individual, but the façade isn't bought and the ideas fade as quickly as they come. The self thought is the prime culprit behind the appearance of struggle and suffering. Strife is only a passing impression registered in peaceful, empty awareness. The only thing that can be said about suffering with certainty is that it will pass(as with any other appearance).

THE "SPIRITUAL EGO"

If anyone ever tells you that they're "enlightened", you'd better watch out. When an apparent person makes this claim for themselves (and conversely claims that others don't have it), this often puts whatever they do beyond reproach and sets up an duality—master and servant. If they're abusive, "it's for your own good". If they demand you destroy all of your other relationships, it's because "they're distracting you from your mission". If they demand that you give all of your time and money, "it's for the cause".

Seekers will worship any idiot in a robe or a gorilla suit who claims that they are enlightened.

Any time one person is put up on a pedestal above another, it's a denial of the truth of oneness.

When it has been claimed that someone has transcended the ego how can they exhibit the petty and tyrannical tendencies that some "masters" do? It's because their "enlightenment" is really just an idea. The self idea is still seen as a reality to them and they act accordingly. They might think that, since they had a "special" experience, they have transcended morality, right and wrong and decency.

Not so. Oneness is lived in the now, not just thought about and talked about. In action, this can be seen as not claiming special status, and as treating "others" with kindness and understanding. How could it be otherwise? Because those "others" are you. In essence, there is absolutely no difference.

One awareness illumines and gives rise to all life. Nothing appears apart from it. Spiritual or religious authoritarian structures don't negate this truth but stand as expressions of ignorance. No one can stand between you and God/being, as *you are That*.

Beware of those who claim to be closer to truth/God than you are—it's simply not possible.

E.T.

I read *The Power of Now* by Eckhart Tolle around 2001 and found parts of it quite compelling. He had some good points like "You are not the mind" and the story of the person who considered themselves a beggar and found that they had been sitting on a chest containing a great treasure all along.

Also compelling, at the time, was the idea of the "pain body"—the suffering collected in the psyche that could, at times, take possession of a person. This idea gives further credence to the idea that suffering is real and even seems to embody it, making it seem like a solid thing. As a concept, it seemed to hold a lot of water, but, when presently looked for directly in experience, all that can be perceived is an empty, cognizant space in which all of manifestation, including thoughts, feelings and sensations, arise and disappear. All things are only ideas. In reality, there is no thing, only *This* that I am, that you are.

Tolle also had a dramatic story of suffering and awakening that I was, at that time, attracted to. The tale of the selfish him "dying" one night was very appealing, as I considered myself such an ego-bound being and yearned for the enlightenment experience that I thought would bring release. That release is only the realization that no such separate self ever existed.

I was so smitten that I considered flying to California to see him. I started researching ticket prices and found some for a talk of his. The audience was separated into circles, the idea being, I suppose, that the closer to him one was, the more likely that one would be bathed in his "radiant enlightened being presence".

The outer or circle tickets were maybe $60 or so. The next was perhaps $80, and the closest to him, the gold circle, was over $100 per ticket. It seemed to be implied that those in the gold circle might have a better chance at transformation than those further away, because of their proximity to the enlightened one. This was the beginning of my disillusionment with him and the very concept of the special, awakened person. There is no enlightened person, there is only the light of awareness.

Wearing robes or fanciful clothes and speaking gently and slowly have nothing to do with awakening. Ringing bells and burning incense won't bring you any closer to what you are (or take you further away, for that matter). Using colorful language or speaking loudly and excitedly are no less of a sacred expression than sitting silently for several hours. Liberation is realizing that there never was one who needed freeing and that our very nature is complete, total freedom, far beyond the human meaning of that word.

In the appearance, of course, every form is unique and different but all arise only in awareness, which is the common ground of everyone and everything. To worship one form over another is folly. The intangible source of form is always present, it just gets missed in favor of a thought story of separation. There is no self involved in any of this. There is no ego, period.

THE ABSOLUTE AND THE RELATIVE (PERSONAL) VIEW

The absolute view is the most basic, elemental view possible. It is pure perception, free of commentary. There is no choice or preference with it, which is why our true nature is always at peace—all things are seen with equanimity. It isn't even a perspective as all apparent perspectives arise within it and don't limit it at all.

The relative perspective is the thought story that arises within the absolute view. It is always from a specific viewpoint, based on a particular interpretation of a very limited experience. It describes characteristics and limitations and, if believed to be real, is the source of suffering and the feeling of separation. What we generally call "reality" is a verbal description of something that doesn't actually exist!

The personal view can pause at any time and the absolute is always present. As an experiment, you might want to pause the thought story for a moment and see if you disappear or cease to exist. The outcome of this experiment proves that one's self-being, is not a concept. This realization can be expressed as *I am,* though it doesn't need to be. It is pre-thought and pre-verbal.

It is all one movement. You were never a part or apart.

The personal is only the appearance of the absolute.
The illusion of multiplicity is just the surface ripples
on the infinite ocean of being.

NO MORE OR LESS

No appearance is more or less perfect—every appearance is impeccable at its job. This might stand contrary to the belief that some things are "right" and some are "wrong". If the message of Advaita is true, no appearance is ever on its own or separate in any way; everything is ever only part of the whole.

Seeing this means the end of guilt *and* the cessation of judging. How can you pass judgment on something that isn't apart from you, is in no way separate from you and has no independent existence, no free will? Only the imagined separate self can appear to judge and its conclusions are meaningless. One is often harshest on oneself but whatever arises can't be helped. Of course the self idea is the main culprit but the appearance of that isn't in any entity's hands.

John Wheeler says that the seeing of the non-existence of the separate self is the end of suffering. I guess that just means that one realizes that there is no personal element to what arises—it's not something we have control over, so why sweat it?

Both the ideas of free will and pre-determination are in reference to a supposed independent individual—is there really such a thing at all? Once again, it's the case that neither concept is up to the task of describing the uncomplicated, spacious presence that *is*.

IMAGES

An image may arise of oneself being some sort of "enlightened master". Another thought may arise that is contrary to the image that you have of "yourself". Anything can appear, regardless of what is expected. It is in seeing the appearance (especially thought forms) as real that the trouble starts. Thoughts are just descriptions of the indescribable. An idea will never encapsulate or understand being.

First comes perception, then thought arises to interpret what is perceived. It's obvious that the description is never the thing. Perception is whole and one. Thought attempts to break it down to understand it better. That which is whole can never be divided but thought can make it seem so. Thought is also an expression of that wholeness but, regardless of what it describes, it never depicts reality, only an interpretation of appearance. It isn't thoughts themselves that are troublesome; it's the belief in them, the acceptance of them as real, that makes them seem problematic.

Everything is fine. All that happened is that a bit too much attention was paid to thought and the natural presence that is the common thread through all experience was missed. Thought arises in being but comes and goes—being is eternal. It is being that is giving rise to and perceiving these words right now. See for yourself.

MULTIPLE CHOICE

Which of these appearances is/was more sacred?

A. The Dalai Lama
B. A bum covered in his own (or somebody else's) puke
C. Hitler
D. Jesus
E. Geraldo Rivera
F. Charles Manson
G. Eckhart Tolle
H. The Pope
I. Gautama
J. A suicide bomber
K. Deepak Chopra
L. None of the above.

If you answered "Deepak", you were right! Just kidding (of course), no appearance is more sacred than another.

PERSPECTIVE

From the viewpoint of science (knowledge), the body is a material object that is solid, meaning "real". It is born, exists for a while and then dies/disappears. Part of the body is the brain, which, in the view of science, is the seat and source of consciousness. No brain, no consciousness.

To consciousness, the body is an intermittent appearance, it's there sometimes and at other times it isn't. It isn't seen as a solid thing but received as changing sense impressions, altering from moment to moment. The mind is merely thoughts that arise and disappear, sometimes there, sometimes not. So neither the brain nor body would be seen as having an independent reality.

The confusion of self with the body/mind hinges on the concept of being these things. The person who accepts this identification as being true is merely another thought. When this is seen, the identification is no longer believed in—there is no one to believe such a thing.

We've been told many things and take them to be the truth. Why not look directly for ourselves? How can someone else's story be more important than our own direct experience?

WHO AM I?

I AM.

This does not need to be verbalized.

The images that appear—they are a movement within my emptiness. Their essence is nothingness.

The images have no existence of their own apart from me.

Thought describes them as having an independent reality, but it itself, is just another appearance.
The essence of every thing is the indescribable and concepts cannot describe that, though they can point to it.

Regardless of what seems to happen in the appearance of life, *being* is untouched and unharmed.

Death is not the end; birth was not the beginning.
Timeless, eternal oneness is present now.

NO LINES

Don't let words fool you; there is nothing apart from being. Look now at what is seen. Are there any lines indicating apartness between what appears? Labels imply demarcations but, when looked for, no dividing lines can be found. Awareness and the perceived are one and only one. Looking directly, this is easy, only thought makes it seem complicated.

What is present right now? This is the real. Everything that is seen is just the shape of the shapeless. "Problems" are only concepts. Looking now, no problem can be found. All is well.

HOW MANY MORE BOOKS DO I NEED TO READ?

None. Awareness will never be more complete than it is right now. No amount of reading or intellectualizing will change your present reality as being. No experience is needed. Enlightenment stories are no truer than any other form of fiction. Waiting for an awakening event is like the sun hoping to someday be bright. It is already the case. Only the idea of a separate self seems to obscure this fact.

Tales of "enlightenment" seem to keep the conceptual self looking to an imagined future where the believed-in entity will "get it". These stories have no more reality than any of the other fables woven by thought. Perfect completeness is present right now.

There's no point in trying to give the imagined pseudo-entity "tools" to discover itself: it doesn't exist and (therefore) it has never done and can never do a thing.

JOY

Such a joyful thing to know this:
What is to be done?
Who is to do it?
It is a song of freedom that is never ending.
No chain was ever forged that could hold being.
It cannot be bound or caged by anything; it is the space in which every "thing" appears.
It is a sun that can never set.
Always, I AM.
When I sleep, I AM.
When I eat, I AM.
When I play, I AM.
When I work, I AM.
It is only because I AM that anything seems to exist.
The images that arise are not under any "one's" control.
Every thing that appears is a complete expression of oneness.
"I" have never done a thing.
This is true freedom—limitless while appearing as manifestation.
It doesn't matter if this is known or not—it is the case.
Everything is perfect just as it is.
Again—everything is perfect just as it is.

SHORTEST POINTERS IN THE WORLD

One
Whole
Unbroken
Love
Not two
Non-duality
Advaita
I AM
It is as it is
What is
No-thing
Not-a-thing
Wholeness—oneness—emptiness—sentience—awareness—consciousness.
Life is a dream

FIXATION

Thought doesn't negate being, though there can be a fixation on thought and the presence in which it arises is missed. One common thought is that "Wholeness has disappeared; I am 'me' again". Of course no such thing as a me ever existed but the idea may seem to be a reality at times. It will pass—all thoughts do. The me, being only a concept, has never and can never do a thing. Belief in the idea of isolation is a dream (or, frequently, a nightmare) that appears in whole and awake being.

Nothing will ever be more perfect than this moment, regardless of what is appearing. More and less are simply concepts. In thought's imaginings, forms are broken into sub-forms and further broken down after that. That's why all of the thought-based religions that purport to try to bring people together end up making more and more sects and divisions. All the time, all that appears is perfect, complete wholeness. No thing can appear without consciousness and consciousness can't appear without undifferentiated awareness.

Try to slip a crowbar between awareness and the objects it perceives. Attempt to pry them apart. Can you? Of course not: they were never separate. It's all one unbroken whole. Consciousness is on and off but being never fades.

NO CRITERIA

No criteria have to be fulfilled for you to be. Every quality or state arises in the clear field of knowing, the presence that one is. Thoughts and forms effortlessly come and go like clouds blown by the wind. It's nothing personal, just the one (not-a-thing) expressing itself as the infinite myriad of possibilities (everything).

In the dream of space/time the passing appearances are seen as having an independent reality of substance and duration. Looking reveals that all that can be directly known is present, all other times and places are merely concepts.

The thought story is often mistaken for the truth, but an idea has never described the actual, although thoughts can be used to try to point in its general vicinity. Being precedes and supersedes conceptualization. The thought story is like a ticker tape running alongside (within) perception trying to narrate what arises. Usually more emphasis is put on it than all of the rest of experience and the tale it spins is believed wholeheartedly. Part of this yarn is about a me, and what must be done to achieve wholeness. This character is entirely fictional and nothing can be added to what one is.

The self idea has never generated a single thought—how could a thought think? What is the implication of this? Everything that has ever appeared has been *being* manifest, regardless of the conceptual narration that accompanies it.

KNOW THYSELF

There is a memory of hearing this statement and the thought would arise: "I don't understand what they're talking about". There was the very strong conviction that something was missing. The trick and joke of it all is that the feeling of lack and thoughts of confusion arose in pure, undivided being and were simply an expression of it. Every appearance is an expression of the absolute.

To fight against something is to empower it. Has the war on drugs worked, or the war on poverty or terrorism? War is always based on ignorance—us versus them, me versus it. Thought is that which seemingly fragments wholeness when its constructs are believed in. Of course this fracture is only a concept: all appears in the peaceful light of being.

Am I:
A name or a form?—Passing thoughts?—A profession or hobby?—A conformist or revolutionary?—A feeling or an emotional response?—An American or an Arab?—A body in a world?—A spirit in the material universe?—A saint or a sinner?

No—all of these identities are conceptual and subject to change. By definition, what you are must never leave you. What is always present in one's experience? The you that is constant is what you really are. You can't lose or gain yourself though the thought story (dream) can convince you so. This is really good news!

Though the thought may arise that you know yourself, you cannot know yourself as an object of knowledge. You are not an object. There is no such thing as an object apart from a subject—all divisions are only conceptual.

AN ALIEN ENCOUNTER

The first humans to travel outside of the solar system were on their interstellar journey when they received a signal of unknown origin. It was coming from an empty point of nothingness at the heart of a nearby nebula. Perplexed, they decided to investigate. As they got closer to the source of the transmission, the onboard computer was able to decipher part of the message: "---come--in----------"

They debated for hours the meaning of the message—was it an invitation from an advanced alien race? Was this spot of nothingness a portal to another universe? After considering all conceivable possibilities they unanimously voted to continue on their original course, away from the singularity.

When the thrusters were applied, they found they were caught in the gravitational pull of the non-object and nothing could break them loose. The computer finally completed its analysis: the void was a black hole. It also finished decrypting the broadcast: "Welcome to inevitability."

Oneness, reality can't be escaped from. Though "you" may not understand the message at first, being, your being, is inescapable. Don't sweat it, enjoy the journey.

"ONE"

On an uncharted island, in the middle of a tumultuous sea, there was rumored to be a great treasure, guarded by a Cyclops called "One". On hearing this, a large group of ambitious men became greedy to have this treasure, which was described as being beyond description. They set sail and, for thirty long years crisscrossed the oceans of the world, looking everywhere One's island was reported to be.

Eventually, on a tip, they found a small, unassuming atoll. Their excitement swelled as they set foot on shore. They brought all of their slaves and beasts of burden along to help them carry what was assured to be the greatest (and, therefore, bulkiest) prize in the world.

Through the evening mist, they could see the mouth of a gigantic cave. Being men (and, therefore, hating monsters), they sharpened their swords and readied their muskets and thought to themselves: "Tonight a Cyclops will surely die!" They lit their torches and worked themselves into a fervor. The lust for gold and blood filled their hearts.

They charged into the cave and saw the bulky form of One, laying next to a smoldering fire. Otherwise, the cave was empty and certainly had no trace of loot. In their rage, they screamed out: "Where have you hidden it, you monster?"

One slowly sat up and turned his head to look at them. His eye was the most beautiful, sparkling gem that they had ever seen and it glowed iridescent in the torch-light. It had an almost hypnotic effect on them and, as they looked at each other, they began to fade and become transparent.

One spoke: "Ah, another dream of mine—it felt so real that it woke me..."

The men disappeared from sight; after all, they were only figments of One's dream. The cave, island and form of One also disappeared, leaving only the shining eye.

In life, the dramas can feel so real and be so compelling. In reality, it's all just the dream of one. It is a waking dream that happens in perfectly lucid awareness.

THE PRESENT OF AN ILLUSION

Taken as a whole, life doesn't produce any illusion. Perception arises in the clear field of knowing. Thought appears to try to break this wholeness down into bite-sized chunks, to make experience more easily digestible. Its descriptions are often mistaken for reality but, no—unbroken oneness is all there is. No conceptual label will ever peg it. Concepts are only an expression of it but shouldn't be confused with truth. In seeing this, thought is allowed to arise however it does, and it is known that it has no bearing on what's real.

Thought is a great storyteller. It's so good at spinning a convincing yarn that its tales are seen as absolute reality. When looked at directly, it is seen to be intangible, intermittent and more fickle than the wind but, when mistaken for actuality, its conceptions are taken as gospel.

Watch it play and enjoy the game—the you that would control it is also only a thought.

LIFE CAN'T BE BROKEN

Observer and observed, perceiver and perceived, knower and known, awareness and objects of awareness, consciousness and its content and any other conceptual, dualistic divisions are entirely unreal. There is only observing, perceiving, knowing, awareness and consciousness, as a single, unitary movement.

How does one know if this is understood on a deeper than intellectual level?

Suffering ceases.

Every living being appears in whole awareness. Every depressive, suicidal, desperate person has no other reality than that essential sentience. Suffering comes from a misconception of one's identity: that one is an object—a physical body with thoughts that arise within a brain inside of it. These thoughts, when mistaken for reality, cause various forms of false identification that lead to misery.

Be still and know that you are not a body or a thought. Know that nothing you've ever believed about yourself is true. Without the knowing-awareness, no body, mind or apparent universe could appear. Isn't this obvious? This is what you really are and it is free of problems and identifications.

A GOOD LAUGH

All that has ever appeared is oneness. Thought, like a mantra, repeats: "This isn't it, this isn't it..." or "Things shouldn't be like this", and accepts this story as a fact. Any talk of awareness and the objects of awareness or consciousness and its content, being conceptual divisions, seems to reinforce this idea.

The perfectly open, crystal-clear nature of being has given birth to all ideas and images. The reality of what we are is unchanging, while, in appearance, transformation is unceasing. Mistaking oneself for form, there is attachment and aversion to what arises. This leads to apparent suffering.

In the non-conceptual knowing of being (I am), every thing appears and fades effortlessly. This is the case right now, regardless of ideas of struggle, isolation and separation.

You are not what you think. What you are cannot be codified into a concept. Always (now), absolute clarity is here.

Words can't do justice in describing any "thing", much less that without attributes. Don't worry about words—you don't need them to know who you are. Your existence is not dependent on words or thoughts. You don't need to add or grasp any concepts to be what you are. (In appearance, of course, they have a functional value but we're talking in terms of knowing oneself.)

Anything is possible. Whatever appears is all right—it has no bearing on your flawless nature. You remain unblemished.

I would say your radiant emptiness is the heart of the universe but, in that case, you would also have to be the spleen, the anus, the bushy eyebrows—everything.

Don't let thought trick you with ideas of sacred and not-sacred or any other dualities. *Oneness abides* (like "the Dude" from the Coen Brothers' movie, *The Big Lebowski*).

Let thought try to describe *That* and laugh at the futility of it.

LOVE

Let's talk about that four-letter word that there seems to be so much controversy about. No, not *that* one, I'm talking about love. What does it mean? Is it a glandular thing between humans? Is it the way you feel about a cute, fluffy puppy? What is it?

Love is just another word for oneness. Nisargadatta pointed out that as long as the idea of separation is active, true love is seemingly eclipsed. When there is no more idea of *I* and *you,* there is love. When there is no more thought of *us* and *them,* it is naturally and effortlessly present. Of course it's always present but a concept (the self thought) cannot love, no matter how hard it tries, because, well, *it and what it is descriving don't actually exist.* Only the undivided is real and that alone can be called love.

THE UNCHANGING

Have you ever wondered what the experience of oneness is like? Here's a hint: what you are experiencing right now *IS IT*.

You are not a person, body, mind or any identifiable thing. The belief that you are limited or embodied is just an idea appearing within your pristine presence. You were never born, you don't have a life and you will never die.

Close your eyes and "look". The unchanging is what you are. The sensations that come and go are appearances; what stays is *you*.

There is only one, unbroken awareness, not trillions of separate centers of consciousness as thought might imagine. In the absence of ideation, no fragmentation is conceived.

As 'Sailor' Bob Adamson so eloquently puts it: *What's wrong with right now, unless you think about it?*

Thought can make problems seem to appear out of thin air. Being has no problems. What kind of problem can undivided wholeness have?

The concept may arise that appearance implies separation. What does appearance arise in? Undivided being.

MISCONCEPTIONS

An oft-appearing idea in "spiritual" circles is that, when one's true nature is realized, life will immediately become completely ecstatic and trouble-free. Not so—the play of life goes on. The old Zen saying "After ecstasy, the laundry" expresses this nicely. Thought seeks for a way for what it labels "bad" to be eliminated, but appearance depends on contrast, so, to do away with what is seen as negative is impossible and unnecessary.

One is not a thing. Our nature is clearer than diamond and more open than the sky—boundless, flawless and awake. Look now, it is so.

There is no standardized code of behavior that will work for every apparent person; the idea that there is comes from the belief that being is contingent on behavior.

Right now, nothing is needed to be complete. The me that needs something has less reality than a shadow and appears in perfectly realized being.

You can't "get" this. We can't get what we already are.

Words/thoughts can never describe reality. The only possible uses they have in this is to destroy other concepts that might seemingly obscure the reality that one is, and to point to that which is beyond all concepts and which is present now.

No one can claim authority on the subject of being as no one can be closer to or farther away from what one is. Being cannot be taught by one who has it to another who doesn't, as everything and everyone arises within it; it is shared. Not shared in the sense of being exchanged between two separate beings but shared in the sense of being common to all. There are no "experts" and "novices" in being. As the ground (reality) of everything, nothing is more nor less an expression of it than anything else.

Don't let the words in this book (or anywhere else for that matter) imply separation—there isn't any.

If you think non-duality is about pointers, you're missing the point.

What in the hell is neo-Advaita? Advaita means not two, non-duality. So is there a new non-duality as opposed to an old one? Once again, thought makes distinctions where there are none.

NON-DUALITY

Advaita, non-duality, means absolutely no duality.

"Then why do I perceive so many separate objects?"

The appearances that are perceived aren't outside but within our aware spaciousness and have no other substance than that emptiness. Hence the Heart Sutra says, "Form is emptiness, emptiness is form". One thought (appearance) that arises in this is: "I am a person and there is a world outside of me". This concept may be believed in, but, actually, all there is is perception/seeing/knowing and it is one and whole. Seer and seen, knower and known, perceiver and perceived are all artificial divisions imagined in thought. Reality is too simple for thought ever to grasp.

What are the implications of this? Well, for one—there are no objects. Things can be talked about in functional terms ("The cat threw up on the couch today") but, in reality, only being is real and it appears as everything. The constant appears as the changing, not-a-thing appears as everything.

THE SENSE OF SEPARATION

Sometimes, it is said that the sense of separation is more than a thought. There is also, at times, a discussion of being embodied. Really, the separate self is no more than an unquestioned belief. If one thinks that a thought can't lead to depth of feeling, consider religious beliefs and how they can make one's worldview and emotions center around what is accepted as truth, even to the point of being willing to die and kill for said concepts. It's the same with the ego idea—while it is believed in, it feels so real that to even question it would seem insane but, if one looks at the evidence, all it amounts to is a bunch of perceptions and fluctuating sensory data that are then interpreted to be a concrete, individual entity.

The key understanding of Advaita is that one is not a body, a mind nor any other identifiable thing but the spacious presence that gives rise to all perceptions and experiences. This can easily be seen for oneself right now by looking directly. Are you aware and present? This sentience is the ground and substance of everything.

THE PROGRESSIVE PATH

Advaita does not lead anywhere. How can oneness be twoness to get from one place to another? How can timeless, boundless being improve as an object in time? All thoughts of someone who is getting closer to being or somehow becoming a better expression of it are just ideas appearing in perfect completeness. It's like the old hamster wheel analogy: you can run as fast and as hard as you want but you're still here (there's no place else to be).

Only an apparent form can alter. This change may be interpreted as good or bad by thought. Being/essence is unchanging. There can't be higher and lower being or presence 2.0; emptiness can't become more empty or better emptiness. Awareness of this is the utter end of the progressive path. Being is all there is—there is no place else to go.

THE STATE KNOWN AS CONSCIOUSNESS

No thing can appear outside of consciousness. In the absence of consciousness, such as in deep sleep, there is nothing perceptible. There may be a vague sense of well-being (of which one becomes conscious upon waking) but no sense of time, space or things. Only when consciousness arises, does appearance seem to be. Thoughts then might arise, describing experience as consisting of a seer and a seen world of objects. Under the belief in this artificial (non-existent) duality, apparent suffering and problems seem to arise. When consciousness is absent, all of these seemingly real issues disappear. Why is that? These problems only seem real as long as the imaginary entity is believed in (which can only happen in consciousness).

The reality of being's wholeness is not obscured by the dream-like appearance of consciousness, though belief in arising concepts may make it seem so. In the absence of consciousness no such misconceptions are possible.

In its pristine state, it's said that being is aware but unaware of itself. What self other than itself could it be aware of? Only with the arising of consciousness comes the apparent world of form and what we mistakenly call "duality"(which is really just the appearance of oneness).

"I am" is the statement of consciousness and self-recognition but our true essence doesn't have or need such words. Consciousness will set but the absolute will not.

WHY IT'S NOT WRONG TO ENJOY LIFE

In some spiritual traditions, especially ascetic ones, there is the belief that the appearance (body/world) is somehow evil and pleasure is to be avoided. Celibacy is promoted over sexuality. Often, a bland, moderate diet, just for sustenance, is encouraged instead of a flavorful one. It seems that part of the reason for these restrictions and others like them is that there is a belief in a separate entity that enjoys these things and is tempted away from the spirit by the flesh. But really, who is the enjoyer? What is the enjoyed? Aren't they one in essence? What gives rise to the appearance of sex, food and everything else? God/being/oneness, of course. That is all there is and you are that.

This doesn't equate to a blank check to be a destructive, irresponsible ass: harmful actions should cease with the recognition of the idea of separation (self/other) as being unreal. If there isn't compassion and kindness, then there isn't understanding. Compassion can manifest as a directness that can seem exceedingly blunt but it won't ever be expressed as abuse.

WHAT IS FREEDOM?

Being is freedom. It can't be marked, scratched or bound. It is spacious aliveness. It is what is reading these words right now and that which is aware of the coming and going of all impressions. No matter what experiences arise within it, it is untouched and unharmed. If it was imprinted by perceptions that arise, it would be a still-life, but it is always open and unfettered—look for yourself.

What we're talking about is your true nature. It is not a thing and, therefore, not subject to decay and disappearance; it is ever-present, ever fresh, crystal-clear aliveness. You cannot see this as an object apart from you—you *are* it!

With belief in the apparent dream character as an independent entity, we accept isolation as reality. Who is aware of this feeling of alienation? Being.

With the cessation of belief in the separate self, naked awareness shines, no longer seemingly obscured by the ego idea. Of course the self thought is also an appearance of oneness: being is inescapable.

It's so ironic that this is the one thing that cannot be lost and that the apparent seeker is trying to frantically find. It's like tearing your apartment apart looking for your keys only to find that they were in your hand the entire time.

If you feel like the search is futile and you'll never get this—you're right! You can't find what you never lost.

Water flows naturally downward. Being naturally appears and disappears as form. There is no giant holding up the sky. Titanic efforts are not required to achieve the infinite. No exertion will make you more or less what you already are: boundless awareness.

THE MYTH OF ENLIGHTENMENT

Enlightenment is an imaginary event that will supposedly happen to an imaginary individual at some point in an imaginary future. There is no such thing as awakening. The apparent person who supposedly lacks such a thing is just an idea presently appearing in perfectly lucid wakefulness.

Enlightenment is a dream-event and only has meaning in relation to an imaginary separate entity. When looked for directly (without concepts), this separate self will never be found, just the clear field of being in which consciousness/life appears. No such event has ever happened here or anywhere else; there is no one apart from it for it to happen to and no other time than *now* for it to happen in. Absolute unity (non-duality) is already the case.

Words muddle the issue but, from where you are seeing, how do you appear? As space/emptiness (no thing) that is obviously cognizant (if it not so, these words or any other thing could not appear).

Separateness is an unexamined belief that topples like a phantom house of cards when looked at non-conceptually. Seeing is *always* non-conceptual but, often, thought is mistaken for perception and what is described is taken for reality. All appearances pass but being does not. Appearances are nothing more than the fleeting expression of the eternal.

EXTERNAL AUTHORITY

There are no experts on being. The idea that "someone else has the answers while I don't" is just an unexamined assumption. What would lead us to believe that the Pope or any other "spiritual" authority has a hotline to God that we don't? Did he go to pope school under the direct tutelage of God? Is it the cool hat? It really all just comes down to unchecked beliefs.

Why do we look outside for answers when everything we need is right here, right now? Buddha said: "Be lamps unto yourselves"—not "Make a bunch of statues of me idolizing my personage" or "Create a complex dogma and a priesthood class". Why worship the memory of an apparent person from thousands of years ago when the awareness that shined on and gave rise to their seeming existence is what you are—the only eternal (timeless) reality apart from which nothing can appear?

When the imaginary wall between inside and outside and enlightened and unenlightened isn't believed in anymore, looking to others for what is already present is seen as patently absurd.

No one is more advanced in being: being is all there is.

If there is appearance, then being is present. If there isn't appearance, then questions of being or non-being are irrelevant (as there is no apparent person to ask such questions). All problems seem to have their root in the separate entity that has absolutely no reality. Only oneness is.

OUR NATURE IS CLARITY

The unchanging fact of being is clarity. No matter what arises within it, it remains such. "Awareness" and "presence" are words that point to this reality. It's strange how there is fixation on arising appearance when this abiding essence is so obvious. Why is there often more identification with ever shifting-forms than with absolute, steady, immovable being?

Seeing can't be seen, therefore, the one essential aspect of all perception and existence is usually overlooked in favor of the transient images that arise within it. Who is doing this? No one: it is the game of God.

Happiness/sadness
Pleasure/pain
Light/darkness
Heat/cold
Male/female

Without consciousness, none of these words have any meaning, nor could they appear at all. All things are simply appearances within consciousness and consciousness is an appearance (in tangible form) of being/awareness. "I am" is the basic expression of existence.

In the absence of consciousness, time, space and all other conceptual fabrications are entirely missing. There is no me, you, us, we or them. No up and down, here and there or this and that. This is why all phenomena and even consciousness itself are called "unreal"—they don't abide, they come and go like a dream, they ebb and flow like the tide. That which is real is timeless, spaceless and unchanging. Words will never describe that.

THE EMPTY PAGE

The empty page is what allows all of the words to appear. If the page was already full of words, no more could be added and it would become an undecipherable jumble. The empty page is necessary for any story to be told. How often do we appreciate the book that contains a story that we cherish?

We are the empty space that allows all of the stories to appear. Unlike a book, no matter what tales appear within us, we will not be imprinted. Our space is always clear and ready for whatever arises. Whatever appears is nothing less than our emptiness expressed as form and has no reality apart from us. If we weren't present, then appearance would be absent. If there was no book, no novel could be written.

ERRONEOUS ERRORS

Don't make the mistake of thinking that I have something that you don't. There is no one out there apart from your presence. Presence is one and identical, regardless of what appears in it. The only kind of permanent identity that we might find is that awareness. For there to seem to be shapes, colors, sounds or any perceptible phenomena, this sentience must be present. It is the constant amidst the ever-changing and, if anything can be called self, it's only that.

Time, space and the sensory experiences that are conceptually bundled together under the term "me" disappear every night during sleep, without a trace. Things that are, during waking hours, considered so real have absolutely no meaning in the absence of consciousness. This is proof of the unreality of the waking dream. When consciousness returns, the thought may arise: "I was asleep for eight hours". But, while unconscious (in deep sleep), no such thought, or apparent person to think it, can arise.

Life is a persistent dream, albeit one that constantly shifts and morphs, and this is why it seems so compelling while the appearance is taken as real. If you woke up as a different person every day, with a completely different physical appearance, emotional traits, warts and so on, it would be quickly seen through and you'd figure it out—"Wait, this isn't really *me*". But as the appearance seems to pick up where it left off and the same fuzzy face is in the mirror in the morning, there is often a belief that this appearance is what you are.

Isn't it obvious that what you are, your true essence, must be ever-present?

What's always present? One's absence as form.

One's absence as form (emptiness) is what allows existence to appear. Without the clear, open space of awareness, nothing would be able to appear. When consciousness is not present, one is still absent as form.

WORDS DON'T STICK

Trying to collect words that one thinks describe reality is futile—do you actually see what they're pointing at? Repetition and understanding of the most perfectly worded description of non-duality has absolutely no effect on the truth of your identity. A word or collection of words can never bring you closer to what you are.

Don't worry about words; just notice the profound clarity of the space in which they arise—the seeing is the space and that which appears in it.

Being is non-verbal. Words and concepts arise later to try to describe what is perceived. They are not necessary, nor do they interfere with what is. They are just another expression of that which is beyond all descriptions.

No sooner are words uttered or thought than they blow away on the wind, leaving the clarity that gave rise to them highlighted, in stark relief, as all there is. The resplendent emptiness of your nature can't be avoided, regardless of what appears in it. Take a peek.

IDENTIFICATION

During a dream, we often become so identified with the happenings in it that strong emotions of fear, loss, sadness and happiness arise, as if it were real. The same thing happens when we watch a movie and feel drawn into the predicaments and triumphs of the protagonist. This perceptive mechanism also creates a feeling of identity with the body/mind that appears in the waking dream.

A dream and what we call waking reality are both appearances in—or perhaps more accurately—appearances *of* consciousness. The only difference between the two is that the waking dream appears more persistent: it seems to pick up where it left off. And just as a dream is sometimes not seen for what it is, despite its inconsistencies, life has the same engrossing quality as long as there is identification with what appears (especially the body/mind—me).

When it is clearly perceived that the body, the mind and the world are simply fleeting appearances in constant awareness, it is seen as futile to identify with the ever-changing and disappearing forms. The field of awareness is all-encompassing: if anything can be called "I", it is only that. In this you can rest as what you always have been, free of the apparent insecurity of a thought-based identity.

WHICH SIDE OF THE WALL ARE YOU ON?

First off, there is no wall, but, when there is belief that one's existence is limited to a particular body/mind appearance, there definitely is a strong sense of separation.

Arising simultaneously with this idea of "me" is the concept of "others", outside of me. It seems that, between these two thoughts, there is some sort of divider or demarcation. This impression arises because of the idea of isolation and, in the absence of such thoughts, the oneness that is always the case is obvious, naturally and effortlessly.

Words in no way change or harm this ever-present reality, but, if the thought stories that arise are mistaken for truth, then there can be, for a time, the feeling of being a particular person.

From this idea of being apart, there can appear to be a reaching out to the other, over the wall, so to speak. Lots of thoughts can arise about how the conceptual other should be dealt with.

All the while, there is no other, only *This*.

This is all there is and, in its absence, no ideas of self and other could appear.

This, that is reading these words right now is the exact same *This* which is typing these words right now.

THOUGHT FABLE

Nisargadatta said (I am paraphrasing): "You think that you are a body born into the world but, in reality, the world is born into you." It's a poignant pointer. The idea of being a limited being is nothing more than a thought form taken to be true. After such a thought has come and gone, you will still *be*. What are you? No-thing.

Not being a thing and, therefore, not having definable perceptible qualities, what problems can you have?

Being boundless emptiness, to which a concept of limitations has no meaning, what dividing line marks your horizon?

If you were not, no thing could appear. Every possible appearance is simply an expression of your registering openness.

MY STORY

I could tell you a story of how I "got it". I could tell about a special moment when everything fell into place and all questions disappeared. I could describe an experience of oneness with the universe or of being overcome with a feeling of unconditional love. What would the point of that be? Such a tale would only have meaning in relation to an imaginary someone to whom such an event supposedly *happened* (note the past tense). In the end, such stories just lend credence to the idea that what is isn't good enough and that one should look forward to some future event (or memory of a past event) for completeness.

Right now, clarity *is*. No imagined past or future event will make it clearer than it is. Awareness must be present for anything to appear. Since existence is arising, it is proof of the reality of being/awareness. There is no being apart from this.

You are not a human being—that's just another story. You are no identifiable thing. This is why looking to the appearance (including thought) for answers to the question of your identity never leads to answers or an end to the questions.

The clarity that you really are has no questions. It is

self-evident and without doubt. It is not harmed or bound by the transient forms (including thoughts) that arise within it. This is the timeless truth of what you are.

Once again, the word is not the thing. That which is aware of words and everything else is the unborn, undying principle—the only reality.

BORING, MUNDANE REALITY

It would appear to be a shame how most of life's amazingly extraordinary phenomena get labeled as ordinary or mundane. Such labels as these betray an intellectual (thought-based) sense of alienation and the conceit of familiarity. As a child, before experience is dominated by a feeling of re-cognition, the appearance of life is met with naked wonder. Every mysterious, miraculous manifestation is naturally respected as being, ultimately, unknowable (not an object of knowledge).

Later (of course it's really only *now,* silly!), as labeling starts, this feeling of amazement at what is appearing gives way to the idea that one has seen it all and the ever-fresh, minute details are ignored in favor of dull, blanket assumptions that pretend to describe what is seen. This is called, by turns, being an adult and knowing. It is also a form of living death.

If one isn't awestruck by whatever is presently appearing, it indicates that fixation on thought (memory) is impeding clear seeing. The field that this and all realizations appear in is transparent and alive with sentience and the source from which all experiences and the mystery of the universe flows. This cannot be lost, regardless of what any thought story says.

WHAT WORDS WILL COME NEXT?

Who knows? They will arise as all forms do from the indescribable emptiness of being. There is no self-involvement with what appears as there is no (separate) self to be involved. The infinite mystery expresses itself in unexpected ways.

If there is belief in a me that is the source of thoughts and actions, then there may also be a belief in individual selves who have seen through their individuality (the idea of enlightened beings) and whose thoughts, therefore, are now different and "charged by stillness" or some such nonsense.

All thoughts arise from emptiness, even the thought that a me is the origin of thinking. Thoughts arise within presence and are either expressed or not. There is no distinction to be made between enlightened people thoughts and unenlightened people thoughts. The idea that there could be such a distinction is just another concept, effortlessly and selflessly appearing in awareness.

IS IT POSSIBLE TO "LIVE A LIFE" COMPLETELY WITHOUT SUFFERING?

What is the source of suffering? Don't rush to answer this, it's worth looking into.

What is suffering? Isn't it a thought or a feeling that things aren't the way they should be? Isn't the root of it the idea of a me that is apart from everything else, that must therefore strive and struggle to make things right?

When the self idea isn't believed in, then what is naturally witnessed? Sensations, perceptions and experiences are arising effortlessly without any personal involvement.

Who are these experiences happening to? No one. No thing. Aware emptiness. Any conceivable thing—you are not.

These words will fade; they aren't important and don't change a thing. What you are watches their disappearance.

You aren't capable of suffering—only a fictional you, or a fictional me is, and it simply isn't real. Just as a mirage of water may seem completely real from one perspective and not appear at all from another, so is the self idea and the sorrow that accompanies it.

WHAT ARE WE LOOKING FOR?

Desires arise: what is sought? Isn't it completeness, regardless of what the current object of desire seems to be?

While the me thought is believed in, there is a natural tendency to want to escape the feeling of limitation that comes with it. To this end, parts of the appearance that are labeled "not me" are considered to hold the key to ending this feeling of alienation.

As one desire is fulfilled, another arises to replace it. While in this mode, the goal is always on the horizon, away from here, away from "me". This is called the state of seeking.

Perhaps, at some point, this "me" idea—the belief in separation—is called into question. It might be seen that it is merely a concept, appearing and disappearing in awareness like all other thoughts.

What remains?

I do.

With the cessation of belief in a seeker who needs to gain something, the sought is found. It's not like an imaginary pot of gold at the end of a rainbow—it was here all along.

In the absence of the self idea, desires still arise. As with all other thoughts, they were never generated by a me.

There is the thought that pleasure comes from external objects, but, when it is realized that all experience is internal (within the self), then one realizes that peace and bliss have always been one's nature—to seek them externally is foolish and unnecessary.

LIFE IS NOT A SHIT SANDWICH

Seekers often accord respect to the idea that life is suffering. It's attributed to Gautama Buddha and is popular in Christian circles, with an emphasis on the passion and crucifixion. If I remember correctly, Nisargadatta, at times, would talk about consciousness as if it were a disease or uncomfortable medical condition, like a weepy case of the clap.

Some might call "Foul!" but I would like to describe what I consider to be the success in finding happiness in the appearance, as the appearance.

Firstly, do what you want to: follow your bliss. If you have a dream, live it. Take advantage of the unreal, elastic nature of appearance. Ideas like "It must be done *this* way" or "Duty demands this" are arbitrary. The belief in a solid, external reality insures much bumping of the head against walls that are purely imaginary.

Secondly, appreciate what you have. Appreciate the treasures that come to you and the challenges that arise while following your heart's desire. Keep your mind open to things working out in ways different than you pictured that may be better than you could have imagined or hoped. If you aren't thankful for what you've got, it's as if you have nothing at all!

Life gives rise to challenges that call our false beliefs into question. These are one of the greatest blessings it offers. If we see through the false, then we are no longer encumbered by it. If you see that the heavy burden that you've been lugging around isn't real, it's a great relief!

It is not a sin to be yourself or enjoy life!

If either or both of these suggestions are totally thwarted and you find yourself crushed in the bottom of a ditch, either metaphorically or literally, you can take solace in the realization that "this too will pass". All experience is fleeting; the simple stability of timeless being is not.

FUNCTIONAL POINTERS

Though the absolute reality of what we are is stable and unchanging, in apparent relativity, there seem to be choices to make that affect our quality of life. These pointers address a couple of those:

At one time, this experience seemed besieged by negative thoughts for what seemed like an extended period of time. Eventually, the thought arose: "What happens if I just be in the present (all there is) and don't think about past and future?" And, instantly, all apparent problems and suffering were gone! Don't worry: *Be*. Try it if you'd like.

Consciousness/life is just like Goldilocks' porridge: though some times it may seem too hot or too cold, it's really just right.

What we take into the body affects thinking on the phenomenal (apparent) level. In terms of the appearance that is the body, diet is *extremely* important and affects every aspect of its health.

All there is is God. No matter how rough life feels at moments, there is great consolation to be taken in this.

THE FIRST LIVING ROBOT

Scientists had worked diligently for decades, trying to develop a machine that was convincingly human. Into its database were put responses to any conceivable question or statement. It was programmed to comb its own hair and whistle while it read the paper. It was also given "memories" of a life it had supposedly lived.

As an experiment, it was put in an apartment in a large metropolitan area. The researchers who had created it would come and visit it as self-described work colleagues. They would ask it questions to see how well the façade of being a person was emulated.

"Who are you?" they would ask.

"I am me."

"How is it that you come to be here?"

"Through my own efforts and personal decisions."

"Who is responsible for this life that you are living?"

"I am, of course."

They were pleased, as it seemed to accept as an

absolute reality the fact of its personhood.

One day, after answering their usual battery of questions, the robot posed a question of its own:

"Who are you?"

THE EASE OF NOT KNOWING WHAT THE HELL YOU'RE DOING

There is a beauty to living life in the moment, not needing to know what comes next. Of course it's impossible to be anywhere else other than this moment. With no clear idea of what should arise, whatever apparently happens is met without the resistance which would come from a "me" who believes itself to be separate from what appears.

Only in thought is one state or thing considered better than another. That's why suffering ends when there is no idea of what should happen—everything is the only way it can be. Appearance is simply the perceptible expression of source.

Knowing (thinking) isn't required except in a few practical instances in the movement of life. If thinking happens, it is also only a manifestation of this wholeness and, therefore, not a problem.

What one is is never lost or found but omnipresent (the only presence). Without the formless awareness that is the core of any experience, what we call "life" could not appear to be. This is what we are. It is not a thing but to call it nothing is also not accurate. It predates the arising of any words of concepts and is necessary for them to arise. It is also beyond and inclusive of any conceptual dualities such as everything/nothing or emptiness/fullness.

Nothing (including any thought) has ever appeared outside of or apart from this singular, nameless principle. It is nothing less than the sole reality. In the absence of an imaginary person (a concept) seeming to try to understand and constrain it with concepts, there is freedom, peace and joy. This is the natural state of being.

Making this into a mental image and seeking it is an exercise in futility: it is here right now ("here" meaning the kernel of all experience—awareness).

Non-conceptual being is the epitome of ease. In the presence or absence of thought, its reality is undeniable. There is no need to accept any concepts as true or false. No mental stance is necessary. Identification with ideas won't bring one any closer to the truth of what you are, nor will it, for that matter, take you away from yourself. Being is unconditional.

YOU ARE NOT A VICTIM

All conceptual identities are false. You are not a thought. All stories and ideas of who or what you are are entirely fictional. The boundless reality that you are can't be understood or explained with concepts. The infinite cannot be boiled down to finite fabrications.

"I am unconscious." What a silly thought! Where could such an idea possibly appear other than within consciousness?

Thoughts in themselves aren't problematic; it's only the belief that they represent reality that makes them seem so.

All relational notions have at their core the assumption of division. Of course these ideas only arise within undivided wholeness, just as everything else does. Though fragmentation is imagined and believed to be the actual, all there is is one inseparable field of being.

Anything that comes and goes—you are not. You are not any thought, form, sensation, experience, perception or even consciousness itself, which is transitory.

There isn't anything apart from essential wholeness, call it what you will. There never has been a separate life or an individual death. Thoughts project a weight and gravity to the passing images that appear in awareness, attaching great significance to them. In reality, all is one and the perceptions and experiences that arise are simply the manifestation of this unbroken oneness. It is all that has ever been, ever was or ever will be—it is all there is. Different times and separate things are just thought's erroneous interpretation of that which cannot be fractured.

WHY PSYCHOLOGY IS BULLSHIT

The main aims of psychology seem to be to make the self-image more comfortable and to help it function better within the framework of society. In humanistic psychology, there is the added aim of helping the "individual" find integration and happiness. The problem with these approaches is that the "me" idea itself is never questioned. The self-image/ego is merely a concept arising in present awareness. It isn't real. What is the point in trying to fix something that doesn't exist? Can you fix something that isn't there? The fact that so many people go to therapy for decades and still consider themselves broken seems to point to the fact that it's impossible. This isn't to say that, if you think that you're hearing voices in your head or suffering mental anguish you shouldn't seek help. By all means do. But seeing the self idea in context frees one from most, so-called mental problems immediately.

What does exist? Is there anything that isn't a concept? Of course. When thoughts cease do I cease to be? Of course not. Being is non-conceptual and independent of any beliefs about one's personal identity. For there to be any ideas about anything, there must be awareness. What problems does crystal-clear awareness have? None are possible.

NO ONE CAN LEAD YOU TO YOU

As long as there is the idea of someone who is awakened and someone who is asleep, thought is weaving illusion. Any concept of an us and a them is patently untrue. Laboring under this falsehood, one seeks answers in the appearance, usually from people who are acknowledged authorities on the subject.

The clearest thing that could be said on this matter is "You don't need me". In the appearance, many make their living by convincing others that they are indispensable. A few that come to mind are politicians, priests and psychologists. Don't expect many of these professionals to tell you that you don't need them...

Wholeness was never lost, so, the idea that someone else can either bring you back to it or teach you techniques and tricks to regain it is laughable.

The separate self that makes life seem so filled with grief and anxiety is nothing more than a passing thought, like all of the others that move through consciousness. These thoughts aren't under the control of any private self but flow from the same primal source that all experience does. This is all there is.

THIS, JUST AS IT IS, IS HEAVEN

Bliss or heaven could be thought of as the state of non-fragmentation. When the self concept is believed in, there is a feeling of disjointedness and struggle; there is an impression of brokenness.

Nothing is broken.

Nothing is apart.

This is an easy explanation of why there isn't an individual life or death: there is no separate self for such a thing to happen to.

All there is is oneness. Within this aware presence, images arise and move and play. Part of this movement is thought which interprets the play as being composed of many separate elements. Really it is always only one, though.

It isn't the case that in life we're apart and in death we're together—wholeness is indivisible. There never has been anyone, anything or any thought apart from that. The perceptions that arise that get tagged with so many labels don't change this fact.

Wholeness can't be understood through a belief

system—it's too simple and all-encompassing. No matter how hard "you" look for it, it can't be escaped.

THE OLD WIZARD

There was a wizened old wizard who lived in a castle overlooking a tumultuous sea. His life had been one long search for arcane, esoteric knowledge. At night, by flickering candlelight, he would search through ancient, dusty tomes looking for the secret of life.

At times, he would read a passage that made him feel that his search was nearing its end, only to be disappointed when the crucial point that would tie everything together never materialized.

As the years passed by, he became more desperate in his quest. Finally, through a traveling merchant, recently back from the Far East, he acquired a huge book, of over ten thousand pages, simply called "The Truth".

He started at the very beginning of the volume and, going methodically from one page to the next, ruminated and pondered each word and phrase until he felt he understood the exact meaning.

More years passed as he read through the mighty document that expounded on every philosophical subject under the sun. He felt his knowledge growing ever more all-inclusive. His goal of perfect

understanding now seemed in sight.
As he neared the end of the book, his vitality left him and he could barely muster the strength to turn the weighty pages, but his obsessive desire to know drove him onward.

He now felt in possession of the wisdom of the ages. In his mighty trained and honed intellect, he could deconstruct and re-construct a perfect functional model of the way the universe—all that was, had been or ever would be—worked.

On his deathbed, he had finally reached the last page. As his eyes scrolled down and he read the final sentence a mad bout of laughter seized him. It read: "But, of course, the truth isn't in any book." This, my friends, was the truth.

THE CHOSEN ONE

In many spiritual traditions, there is the idea of the messiah or chosen one, someone who will bring order to a world that is perceived as being chaotic or out of balance. Many stories and movies also have this theme, for instance, the Matrix and Harry Potter tales. What this concept obviously implies is that everything is not of the source but that, occasionally, one particular appearance is chosen to be its vehicle or act as its representative. This is an erroneous belief.

Every thing that appears is none other than the one, indivisible reality manifesting, and has no existence apart from that. No appearance is more or less important than any other. All there is is that which cannot be named or described, and every perception is only a movement of light within that.

One really demystifying thing to realize is that no one is better than you and that no one is closer to truth than you are: You are that.

There is nothing that can make this moment more divine than it is. No chorus of angels or shining spiritual master needs to appear. The one life flows without beginning or end.

PERSONALIZING TRUTH

I was reading a website the other day where someone was talking about a teacher and said that this person was passing on Ramana Marharshi's "light".

No appearance (of a person or otherwise) owns the light. The light, or awareness, is that which all forms appear in.

If one hears the truth of non-duality from an apparent someone, there might be a temptation to say that that person gave one understanding. Not so. All that happened is that *what is* was pointed out. This reality is always exactly the same as every apparent form arises within it. The realization of this is the end of belief in anything personal.

Yes, there is an appearance of a person and it is absolutely unique, but this can only arise within the clear knowing of being and has no seeming existence without it.

INDIVIDUALISM—A PRACTICE

The message of non-duality doesn't mean that everyone should don grey jump suits and shave their heads so no differences can be seen. What it means is that every varied appearance is already an expression of that absolute principle.

When there is fixation on form, the thought may arise that one needs to follow a certain code of conduct to become fit to represent and commune with the infinite, but when it is realized that the seeing is already wholeness, all urge to conform to a pattern dissipates. Why try to become something else when this is it, when you are it?

No thought-projected image of perfection can match what is.

There is no need to try to change anything. In appearance, change is inevitable and will come of itself, just as the seasons flow effortlessly into each other.

There has never been anyone who ever willed anything, only the play of shadow and light in the timeless eye of God.

There is no possibility of being anything else besides being. Being is not plural but singular and undivided.

This simplicity can be called love.

THE EGO CANNOT DIE

... for the simple reason that anything that isn't real never lived.

You cannot kill the ego. Try to smite the air with a stone and you will hit nothing.

It all boils down to one unexamined or perhaps cherished assumption: that I am apart from life and death. While laboring under this pretext, it seems that every second brings a new struggle. It feels like being in the trenches.

What a relief to find this object of crushing gravity to be nothing more than a passing thought—nothing. While assumed to exist, it feels denser and more substantial than a black hole, but the ego is simply not real.

What is real?

What is real is present right now, day or night, asleep or awake, rain or shine.

Time and space are just misinterpretations of it by thought.

It is something that cannot be grasped but can never be lost.

Search into the endless universe and you will still be it. You cannot find that which was never missing.

FEAR AND HOPE

Fear and hope are the projections of thought into an imagined future.

With the belief that one is a corruptible body and limited mind, fear is a constant companion.

Fear pretends to describe what will come to pass, but if its predictions are noted, it will be seen that things seldom work out the way they were imagined.

Hope is holding on to the idea that things might be better down the road.

Both of these emotions can only arise when the fact of there being no future is missed. Of course all there is is the present, so the scenes painted involving hope and fear are entirely fictional. This isn't to say that these feelings should be avoided—like all others they will arise and pass without any personal involvement, leaving the essence of what we are.

THE BELIEF IN SEPARATION IS THE ROOT OF ALL SUFFERING

War, crime, pollution, terrorism, greed, politics (including organized religion)—how many of these would exist without the idea of a separate self?

Knowing that you are intimately connected to the earth, at one with it, how could you pollute it? Knowing that you would breathe any air you polluted, drink any water you tainted and eat food from the soil you poisoned, would you do it?

Knowing that the awareness that the appearance of "you" arises in is the exact same as your neighbor's, how could you hurt them? Seeing all of the similarities in the appearance—the fact that you both want yourselves and your family to be happy and safe from harm and, knowing that, as being, you are indivisible, how could you cause harm to them without knowing that you're hurting yourself?

The answer is simple: the idea of separation. It lets us think that we are isolated from nature, our fellow human being and even the consciousness that life appears in.

This isn't in anyone's hands—if it was, do you think

anyone would actually choose to live under the veil of suffering and alienation?

Everything that is ever perceived or experienced is the impersonal movement of form within limitless awareness. This is your show; I hope you're enjoying it!

ACCURACY

What thought or group of words most accurately describes the reality of being?

The absence of words.

This isn't to say that words somehow disrupt what is. Everything arises within and is only of that singular primordial principle.

ENLIGHTENMENT—A DEFINITION

If anything could be called "enlightenment", it would only be the lack of belief in an entity that such a thing could happen to.

There is no separate being, only *being*. In the absence of being/awareness, no apparent form, including what gets labeled "the individual", can arise. When the small self is no longer believed in, then what is happening?

Oneness is appearing as all things.

This is always the case, whether life is trouble-free and effortless or when it seems like a struggle. The only apparent difference in these ways of experiencing is the ego idea. When the ego idea is present and accepted as being real, there is suffering and a belief in personal effort, guilt, pride, etc. When the self concept is absent then there is only what is: naked being, and no feeling of individual doer-ship.

There never has been anything apart from wholeness, including the idea that something is apart. What this all boils down to is, regardless of what appears to be happening, nothing is wrong—it is all only the appearance of the sole, unitary reality. There is no ego involved anywhere.

EXCLUSIVITY

Anyone who implies, either through words or actions, that being is somehow exclusive or reserved for the few, is full of shit.

The idea that being is a special experience is pure foolishness. Being is the source of all appearances but it is not a state, condition or any perceivable thing.

Personal merit is not a prerequisite for awakening. The concept of a person, merit, punishment, reward or anything else can only arise in awareness/ wakefulness.

The notion that one is asleep or selfish or sinful or any other such conclusion is an artificial (false), thought-based identity, and such thoughts can only appear in the clear lucidity of presence, without which nothing can seem to be at all.

To be what you are, nothing is needed, and no one can give you to you or lead you to yourself. If you were not, nothing could arise, including questions and seeming answers.

Though there may be a belief that one is lost and a desire to be found, such ideas only arise within the clarity and wholeness that you really are.

The heartbeat of all existence and experience is that which can be labeled awareness, and this heart beats unfalteringly.

UNFETTERED PRESENCE

The projections of thought are what make the infinite seem limited.

If it is seen that none of thought's stories are true, there is a great sense of freedom.

No story needs to be believed, even the idea that "none of thought's stories are true".

Being needs no words to express it. As the false self sense naturally drops away, there is an effortless flowing. The constricted feeling of being a limited self unfolds, leaving only a profoundly simple openness. This unfettered presence is what we are.

The thought story can only ever be temporarily fixated upon: it is bound to fade and with it go all dreams and notions of limitation.

Effort cannot bring one any closer to the infinite. The infinite is the seeing, regardless of what is apparently seen.

If you were omnipotent, omnipresent, all-pervading—the only reality, couldn't it be fun to pretend that you are other than that?

IT IS!

Perhaps there is the thought that one is an object (body/mind), traveling through space and time, but such an idea is only an appearance within timeless being—you are nothing other than that.

THE VALUE OF WORDS

Everything in this book is a concept.

You are not a concept.

There is absolutely no need to cling to any thought, phrase or sentence. All of the words within this book are absolutely useless and it might be better to crumple the pages until they are silken soft and then use them as toilet paper.

The only possible value they might have is to point directly at that which is seeing these words and which is the unwavering fulcrum, without which the appearance of life, death, anything or nothing whatsoever would be impossible.

THE HEROINE AND HER QUEST

There once was a great heroine named "The Seeker". From birth, she was told that she was the chosen one who was destined to defeat the dragon, Self.

She trained so much with her sword called "Knowledge" that wielding it came as naturally as breathing to her.

It was prophesied that at a certain time she would face the great monster and, as that time drew near, she was filled with anticipation.

She honed her skills, day and night, and imagined every possible scenario of the impending conflict.

She became so single-mindedly obsessed with defeating the beast that it was the only thing in her life that had any meaning.

She read tales of other fights against dragons and of the successes and mistakes of other heroes. She also read of the great relief that came once the dragon was dead and knew that praises would be sung of her for ages to come.

The day of her fight had arrived. It was a cold

day, with not a ray of sun shining through the impenetrable clouds. Her metal armor was frigid against her skin and her sword hand shook slightly with anticipation.

As she neared the lair of the dreaded fiend, she prayed to the gods for victory and promised to serve them for ever more.

Everyone knows that dragons breathe fire so, as she approached the open mouth of the cave, she expected to be buffeted with flames, but none came forth.

She grasped her sword so tightly that her hand turned white and rounded the bend of the entrance.

She was shocked to see, not a dragon, but a large, empty cavern. On the far side, she could see something gently glinting, and approached it out of curiosity.

As she got nearer, she realized that her blade would do her no good and let “Knowledge” drop to the floor with a loud clang.

Before her, she saw an ornate mirror made entirely of ice. In it, she saw a stern-faced warrior, features clenched in a mask of aggression and fear—herself. She took her gauntlet off and, with her bare hand, touched the mirror. As she did, it melted and flowed quickly out of the cave.

After that day, she wandered around the world, sharing the message of the non-existence of self and the uselessness of knowledge to defeat something that wasn't real.

When one associates with the thought image of being a seeker, there is a sense of great drama and deadly seriousness.

When it is seen that the seeker isn't real and that no separate self ever existed, there is peace. This peace is always present; it is merely overlooked sometimes in favor of arising forms.

LIFE IS EASY

...when a tragic story isn't believed in.

Whatever cosmos is conceived of, be it friendly or hostile, isn't real, only the unnamable, all-pervading presence is.

There never was anyone born into a separate life and faced with certain death. There aren't a million and one competing, warring factions struggling for survival. Nothing has ever been in conflict, regardless of appearances.

All such ideas are apparently the result of thought attempting to translate perception, but it is an unbreakable whole that can't be intellectually understood.

Whatever you think you are, at all times and places, complete peace is present. No dream of gain or loss will ever affect the clear lucidity that you are.

This won't be grasped as it can't be dropped.
All attempts to do so are only a dream activity undertaken by a dream character. Being is utterly without conditions and perpetually uncaused.

If there is awareness, then what we are talking about is present. We are nothing more than *that.*

There is no individual dreamer; all ideas of such only appear in perfect wakefulness.

BEING MINDFUL OF "THE MIND"

Trying to know yourself by being aware of the stream of arising thoughts is an outright impossibility. Sit and watch thought for as long as you like and you still won't know any more about your true nature. The real question is, who or what is aware of thinking?

Desiring to change yourself by changing your thoughts is akin to trying to become a different person by changing your socks—thought has nothing to do with who you are.

Without consciousness, thoughts have no meaning; therefore, thoughts are dependent on consciousness. Consciousness would appear to be closer to what you are, but still, it comes and goes.

Without the all-encompassing field of being in which consciousness arises and sets, consciousness has no meaning therefore, consciousness is dependent on being and is nothing more than an expression of it. This is the unchanging reality of what you are: unconditional, timeless and beyond description.

All divisions are only in thought—there is no separation. What you are is not a thing but can be labeled sentience, awareness, being, etc. Within this arises the appearance of all things, which have no other substance than this sentience. But, truthfully, the words are unimportant. Words always imply divisions and distinctions where there are none, so no wonder it can seem confusing if these constructs are believed in. Words will never encapsulate what is. You don't need intellectual understanding to *be* – the being comes first.

Thought weaves stories but can never describe the real—oneness is too simple, and present, to need describing.

Consciousness does come and go but, even when unconscious, such as in deep sleep, there is a feeling of well-being that one becomes aware of upon waking. This well-being is, well—being.

CREATION

Nothing has ever been created apart from oneness—all experience is within.

All creation myths and scientific beliefs regarding the beginning of the universe are merely stories concocted in thought and are equally false. Thought seems to imagine and then posit ends to space and time because it cannot wrap itself around the infinite.

Not one single electron exists except as an appearance in being, which is its only substance. There is nothing besides this singular substratum.

What we call objects are simply a movement within awareness. What we call an individual is indivisible from the rest of life. No thing exists outside of this that I am.

Even to say "within" is confusing as it implies a "without"—that is why language is misleading on the subject. This is too simple to ever be verbalized. No concept is needed—just *be*.

Think as much as you want about non-duality and, when thought subsides, you will still be present.

LEVELS AND DIVISIONS

One plainly dualistic idea is that of higher and lower states of consciousness. Sometimes, this is expressed as Christ-consciousness or cosmic consciousness as opposed to the everyday, common or garden variety. Of course this division is false—consciousness is awareness of contrast. Though the content may seem to vary, consciousness is always the same, registering all that arises. Nisargadatta said (paraphrased): "The consciousness of Krishna and a donkey are the same."

Another example of thought attempting to divide that which cannot be divided is the concept of the chakras, separate energy centers within the body. Also, there are ideologies where the physical body is considered distinct from the soul, the astral body, the causal body and the pain body (Eckhart Tolle).

All of these are artificial, thought-based divisions.

In terms of levels of importance, God is often placed at the top, followed by the prophet, guru, avatar or whatever, then humanity, then, of course, every other living thing on the planet.

All such hierarchies are absolutely unreal. It's just another example of the fragmentary imaginings that arise within thought.

Without belief in such ideas, there is living as wholeness.

With acceptance of these concepts as being true, there is living as wholeness and feeling apart—suffering.

Thought cannot describe oneness, only fragments of perception. Being is all-encompassing and unbroken, regardless of what is concocted in thought. Trying to split it to understand it is futile. *You are it.*

DO YOU KNOW WHO YOU ARE?

This is the crux of non-duality.

When this question of self-identity is answered—wordlessly—seeking is done.

The answer won't be found in so-called "knowledge" or thought—in fact, it won't be found in the appearance at all.

Who is aware? Who sees?

Isn't it the case that the things that get labeled "me" (thoughts and bodily impressions) are just among the many phenomena that are perceived?

Who perceives these things?

Take away your name and you still are.

Take away thought and you still exist.

Take away the bodily impressions (as in sleep) and being does not cease. As the conceptually bundled group of sensations that is called the body ages and changes and even loses parts, you remain the same.

Take away every identifiable thing that could be called "me" and what is left?

Sentience. Within it, all things are registered with equanimity.

Being a seeker, being a person, being a mind within a body within a world—all of these are thought images. What allows them to arise?

Awareness.

What is the source of awareness?

It is source-less and uncaused—it just *is*. Without it, there could be no apparent world of sensory experience. In its absence, no apparent person, with questions of identity, could arise.

When there is a feeling of apartness, of needing *something* to be complete, of being a seeker, where does it originate?

With the belief in separation...

...which arises selflessly in the clear space of being.

Looking directly, this is impossibly simple.

Seeing this conceptually is impossible: a thought cannot see.

You are the seeing.

YEA OR NAY?

So do you believe or disbelieve what has been said? Either is an intellectual stance and has nothing to do with truth. There is the thought that, by finding and adhering to the correct concepts, we will be aligned with the real, but reality, what we are, is non-verbal. It is not an idea and cannot be caught or described by words or symbols. When 'Sailor' Bob and others say "non-conceptual awareness", this is all that they're pointing out.

This is the easiest thing in the world to prove—when thoughts subside, do you disappear? No, of course not. It doesn't take an idea to sustain being—being is the source and only reality of every thing that appears.

Are these words helpful or a hindrance? I don't know. It doesn't really matter. The words have never mattered. They are here to point out the unmistakable essence of life. They are here to point at the obvious existence of sentience but, in themselves, they have absolutely no value. Look for yourself and don't rely on anyone's words. Trying to understand by concepts makes it all seem absurdly complex.

THROW IT ALL AWAY

If you feel like you have learned anything from this book, and I certainly hope you have, you should immediately throw it all away. Knowledge is a useless and unnecessary burden in describing reality. You don't need a boat to take you to the other shore—there is no other shore. You are already here.

Every word implies another thing and there are no objects except as a movement within consciousness. As Ramana pointed out ("Use a thorn to remove another thorn and then throw both away"), it seems that the most effective use of concepts is to use them to obliterate other concepts and then to discard those that remain. Nothing needs to be added to being—it is complete right now, the only "time" there ever has been.

Regardless of what words have been said and what they describe, there is no division anywhere and every "where" is only here. There is no consciousness apart from awareness, no appearance apart from essence, no thought apart from being—no duality.

Who can deny being? Being *is* knowing—not a shallow intellectual understanding but pure knowing itself. Every thing is only a movement of and within the open presence that you are. Why not?

SUGGESTED READING

You Are No Thing by Randall Friend: some robust direct pointing.

Unworldly Wise by Wei Wu Wei: a simple explanation of non-duality in the form of a children's fable.

Already Awake by Nathan Gill. I like the directness of Nathan's approach. The title pretty much says it all.

Living Reality: My Extraordinary Summer with 'Sailor' Bob Adamson by James Braha. Reading this book, I almost felt as if I was with James and his group of friends/fellow seekers and Bob.

Pointers from Nisargadatta Maharaj and **Duet of One: The Ashtavakra Gita Dialogue** by Ramesh S. Balsekar. *Pointers* gives a concise review of the teachings of Nisargadatta and also an idea of what it was like to be around him. *Duet of One* is the Advaita classic *The Ashtavakra Gita* with Ramesh's commentary on the text.

The Collected Works of Ramana Maharshi edited by Arthur Osbourne.

Crest-Jewel of Discrimination by Shankara. Translated by Swami Prabhavananda and Christopher Isherwood. Another abiding Advaita Vedanta work.

Hardcore Zen: Punk Rock, Monster Movies and the Truth About Reality by Brad Warner. A book with some good pointers and a subjective account of the author's search for "enlightenment".

The Ashtavakra Gita and *Crest-Jewel of Discrimination* have some very direct pointing in them. This is mixed with an emphasis on asceticism, which, as far as I can tell, mostly comes from cultural influences at the time they were written. If it's true that there is only oneness and every manifestation is an appearance of that, what does it matter if one wears a loincloth or pants?

LINKS

If you would like to contact me, you can email me at: **moemunee@hotmail.com**.

My blog: **http://blesseddisillusionment.blogspot.com/**

My old website: **www.ashevilleadvaita.info**

John Wheeler's website:
www.thenaturalstate.info

'Sailor' Bob's website: **www.sailorbobadamson.com**

Randall Friend's blog: **http://avastu0.blogspot.com/**

Non Duality Press: **www.non-dualitypress.com**

Urban Guru Café: **urbangurucafe.com**—the home of scores of great podcasts on the topic of non-duality.

CPSIA information can be obtained
at www.ICGtesting.com
Printed in the USA
FSOW01n0948180916
25150FS

9 780956 643292